DISCUSSION PAPER 43

The Proliferation of Anti-Dumping and Poor Governance in Emerging Economies

Case Studies of China and South Africa

XUAN GAO

NORDISKA AFRIKAINSTITUTET, UPPSALA 2009

Indexing terms

Foreign trade
Trade policy
Dumping
Unfair competition
Trade barriers
Trade agreements
Governance
Trade liberalization
China
South Africa

The opionions expressed in this volume are those of the author and do not necessarily reflect the views of Nordiska Afrikainstitutet.

Language checking: Peter Colenbrander
ISSN 1104-8417
ISBN 978-91-7106-644-2

Printed in Sweden by GML Print on Demand AB, Stockholm 2009

Contents

Abstract

Through examination of the alleged rationale of the anti-dumping (AD) instrument, this paper argues that it has little to do with fairness or with level playing fields. AD trade protection enjoys broad political support merely because its convoluted technical complexities prevent all but a few insiders and experts from understanding the reality that underlies the rhetoric, thus enabling inefficient but well-organised domestic producers to safely utilise the instrument to protect themselves from foreign competition, at times in collusion with foreign exporters and with the national AD authorities as a broker. While the best option for AD reform, i.e., complete removal, is not practically available, this paper proposes improving AD's procedural institutions by enhancing the quality of public governance in the formulation of AD decisions by national authorities. It further examines the AD practices and laws of China and South Africa, arguing that poor governance in emerging economies contributes to their prolific use of AD, usually disproportionate to their small share of world imports. These economies already maintain higher tariff barriers than industrial countries, so that without effective steps to ensure better governance to restrain the arbitrary and proliferating use of AD, they may lose out significantly on the gains from the trade liberalisation for which they have been striving for decades.

Foreword

The issues of dumping and anti-dumping have been central to the theory and practice of international trade and trade disputes between trading partners. In this special issue, Xuan Gao unmasks the rhetoric of anti-dumping, whose supposed aim is to offset unfair trade practices and promote international competition. Emerging economies are subject to the same substantive WTO anti-dumping (AD) rules as industrial countries, but, as Gao laments, emerging economies such as China and South Africa frequently adopt AD measures out of all proportion to their relatively small share in global trade. This is so, according to Gao, because anti-dumping is cast in convoluted and complicated technical jargon that gives Chinese and South African producers considerable room to manoeuvre and he sees their actions as being essentially anti-competitive. He recommends two options for the reform of AD rules: a complete removal of AD; and enhancing the governance quality of the AD decision-making process, enhancements that include transparency, stakeholder participation and the rule of law. Gao argues that the low-quality of public governance in AD decision-formulation contributes to the arbitrary and proliferating use of AD by emerging economies such as China and South Africa. Clear articulation of national AD rules (both procedural and substantive) involving all stakeholders and stronger and more effective surveillance of the implementation of the rules by an efficient judicial system are important prerequisites if AD rules are to offset unfair trade practices and foster international competition.

We believe that this contribution will add to the growing and complex debate on international trade rules and illustrates that those countries lacking the technical capacity to decode the complex legal jargon of trade rules will always be at the losing end of the game. What is clear from the case studies is that China and South Africa, because they possess legal and technical skills in trade negotiations, have been able to decode the existing anti-dumping rules and turn them to their own advantage. A closer reading, however, reveals that these counter-responses and practices are in themselves anti-competitive as long as policy formulation on anti-dumping remain less than transparent and judicial review remains inefficient or non-existent. Both China and South Africa may in the end lose out on the gains from trade liberalisation if they continue to rely on the arbitrary use of anti-dumping instruments.

Professor Fantu Cheru
Research Director

1. Introduction

The past two decades have seen, inter alia, three changes in the world trading system: significantly reduced traditional trade barriers such as tariffs, the proliferation of the adoption of anti-dumping (AD) laws and of the use of AD instruments by national governments, and the dramatically increasing contribution by developing countries to that proliferation. AD ostensibly aims at offsetting unfair and anti-competitive trade practices, but a controversial reality underlies the rhetoric. This paper reveals the substantive defects of the AD instrument and proposes procedural improvements in national authorities' AD decision making as a second option for AD reform, since the best option – complete removal – is not yet politically available. By examining the AD institutions of China and South Africa, two major targets of AD but also prolific new AD users, against three criteria of good governance, namely transparency, stakeholder participation and the rule of law, it is found that both countries have relatively poor governance in the AD decision-formulation process. Lessons from China and South Africa are of particular significance to other emerging economies, all of which already maintain higher tariff barriers than industrial countries and face similar public governance problems. Without effective steps to ensure better governance to restrain the arbitrary and proliferating use of AD, theses economies may be at a significant disadvantage in benefiting from trade liberalisation.

The organisation of this paper is simple. The next section rebuts the pro-competition rhetoric of AD laws and reveals their trade protectionist reality from the political economy perspective. Section 3 proposes improvements to the procedural institutions of AD by enhancing the quality of public governance in AD decision formulation by national authorities. It further examines the AD practices and laws of China and South Africa, arguing that the poor governance in emerging economies may contribute to their prolific use of AD disproportionate to their small share of world imports.

2. Anti-dumping: Rhetoric vs. Reality

2.1 The Rhetoric of AD: To Ensure Level Playing Fields by Offsetting Unfair Competition

The alleged rationale underlying AD, i.e., to offset unfair and anti-competitive trade practices, is examined and rebutted in this section. It is argued that the AD instrument has little to do with fairness, nor with level playing fields, and that the discriminatory treatment of the dumped products of foreign companies is not only incompatible with national competition laws but also with the World Trade Organization.

2.1.1 The Economic Rationale of Free Trade and Competition

Without engaging in trade, every person would have to be an autarkist, i.e., she must produce everything (goods or services) she needs to maintain her life – food, clothes, housing, healthcare, etc. Not surprisingly, nobody can achieve expertise in all these fields in a timespan as short as a human life. However, trade makes it possible for one person to concentrate on one line of production (e.g., farming), while another specialises in another line (e.g., housing). This is the law of 'comparative advantage', revealed by David Ricardo (1821) and accepted by many others as a standard economic axiom. (Ricardo 1821; Rothbard [1962] 2004; Samuelson and Nordhaus 1998).

In addition, trade leads to efficient production through competition between all producers of like products in that country. The market for trade rewards and stimulates technological innovation (in the production of both goods and services) that allows the participants, as producers, in the market to satisfy their consumers in the best way and at the same time to achieve the highest earnings (profits) from them in return, and, as consumers, to be best satisfied by other producers (Schumpeter 1943; Mises [1949] 1998: 805; Smith [1776] 1947: book I, ch.ii; Turgot [1774] 1977). Less productive companies and even industries will be killed off, but the rest will drive up the economy and in the best interests of consumers – a ruthless process, from which, however, everybody will benefit over the long run.

2.1.2 AD: A Competition-Distorting and Protectionist Instrument

Dumping and AD are regulated under the Article VI of the *General Agreement on Tariffs and Trade 1994* (*GATT*) and in greater detail under the WTO's *Agreement on Implementation of Article VI of GATT 1994* (*WTO AD Agreement*). Simply put, dumping occurs when the exporting country introduces products into the commerce of the importing country at a price less than the normal value of these products. Normal value basically refers to the price of these products on their home markets or the cost of production in the exporting country.[1] Price setting is a right of private agents generally recognised by all market economies. The WTO law, which basically

1. Article VI (1) of the *GATT* and Article 2 of the *WTO AD Agreement*.

only imposes obligations on and regulates the behaviour of governments, does not prohibit dumping. WTO members are entitled to impose anti-dumping measures (usually in the form of additional duties) against only *condemned* dumping, i.e., dumping which causes or threatens material injury to an established industry in the importing country or materially retards the establishment of an industry in that country.[1]

WTO agreements do not provide any explanation of why the injurious dumping should be condemned and the General Secretariat of WTO indeed acknowledges the existence of controversy.[2] When the *GATT* was negotiated in 1947, countries, including the UK, argued that AD laws were a hindrance to free trade and that the *GATT* should prohibit the imposition of AD duties (Blonigen and Prusa 2004). However, Article VI was finally incorporated into the *GATT* largely at the insistence of the US. (Trebilock and Howse 1999:167).[3] During the *GATT* Uruguay Round and the WTO Doha Round Negotiations, the US and the EC successfully resisted efforts to eliminate or impose stricter discipline on AD to the extent that the Doha Ministerial Declaration promises preserving the basic concepts, principles and effectiveness of the *WTO AD Agreement* and its instruments and objectives (2001:para.28).

The US and the EC regard dumping as market- and trade-distorting practices and unfair competition and thus, in the absence of an international competition regime, dumping has to be addressed through AD measures.[4] A number of economists, while acknowledging various defects in current AD provisions, also consider the convergence of AD rules and competition laws as a solution to such defects (Hoekman and Mavroidis 1996; Messerlin 1994). Nevertheless, as will be analysed below, the AD instrument has little to do with promoting competition. On the contrary, it can and has led to significant anti-competitive consequences by protecting inefficient but usually concentrated domestic producers from foreign competition. Indeed, there cannot be such a convergence option.

First, dumping exists where the 'normal value' of the product exceeds the 'export price'. However, by applying the technically complicated but legally loose methodologies provided in current AD laws of both the WTO and its members, competent national authorities can, and have, easily manipulated the results of AD investigations by artificially constructing a higher 'normal value' and a lower 'export price' at

1. Article VI (1) of the *GATT.*
2. http://www.wto.org/english/thewto_e/whatis_e/tif_e/agrm8_e.htm.
3. Even though the US enacted AD dumping law (1916) much later than several other countries such as Canada (1904), New Zealand (1905), Australia (1906) and South Africa (1914).
4. See, e.g., the US *Trade Act 2002*, Public Law 107–210, sec. 2102(b)(14)(A.); the European Commission: COM (2006) 763 final; and various proposals by the US to the WTO Negotiating Group on Rules such as TN/RL/W/27 and TN/RL/W/35 and the *Doha Ministerial Declaration* (2001: para. 28).

will.[1] Second, even though dumping as defined in AD laws actually occurs, it may well still be irrelevant to anti-competition.

Until the last decade of 20th century, the notion underlying dumping under the US law was 'price discrimination', in particular 'predatory pricing'. Under the US *Robinson-Patman Act 1936* (RPA), sellers are generally required to sell to everyone at the same price.[2] But, as explained by the Supreme Court in *Brooke Group Ltd v. Brown & Williamson Tobacco Co. (1993)*,[3] 'the [RPA] condemns price discrimination only to the extent that it threatens to injure competition ... Congress did not set out to outlaw price differences that result from or further the forces of competition'. The Federal Trade Commission therefore only takes action under the broader antitrust law (Clark 1995) against price discrimination, i.e., that causes or threatens to cause injury to the competition between the seller granting the discriminatory discount and other sellers of relevant products, which is similar to that between domestic producers and dumping foreign exporters.[4] This particular form of price discrimination is also called 'predatory pricing' under the US antitrust law,[5] which was accepted as the rationale for AD by both the legislative and judicial branches. The Senate Finance Committee described dumping as 'pernicious' when drafting the US anti-dumping law in 1979 and the US Court of Appeals for the Federal Circuit, which oversees the administration of the law, termed dumping 'predatory' (Knoll 1991).

Nonetheless, to prove the existence of predatory pricing, i.e., a practice of driving rivals out of business by selling at a price below cost (Hovenkamp 1999:335), a plaintiff in court has to present evidence of the seller's *intent* to drive its rivals out of business. This intent test is essential to courts in determining the impact of dumping on competition and is widely provided for in many countries' competition laws.[6]

In the EU, price discrimination, including predatory pricing, is regulated under Article 82 of the *EC Treaty* as one of the forms of abuse of a dominant position. In other words, selling products to different customers at different prices by a company which does not hold such a position is basically not prohibited. By the same logic, dumping at a price less than cost is also allowed in many other countries, including China and South Africa, as long as the dumping firm is not a dominant one as

1. For the purposes of this paper and for reasons of space, rather than repeat at length the relevant analyses and findings, we simply incorporate some of them by reference (Blonigen and Park 2004; Corr 1997; Eymann and Schuknecht 1996; Feaver 1997; Finger and Fung 1994; Horlick and Shea 1995; Kufuor 1998; Lindsey and Ikenson 2003; Martin 1999; Palmeter, 1995; Vermulst and Driessen, 1997; Waer, 1993; White, 1997).
2. Section 2(a).
3. *Brooke Group Ltd. v. Brown & Williamson Tobacco Corp.* (92–466), 509 US 209 (1993).
4. Price discrimination will also be prohibited if it causes or threatens to cause injury to the competition between the favoured customer of the seller who receives the discriminatory price and the seller's other customers and to the competing customers of the disfavoured purchaser. However, these two forms are irrelevant to the situation of condemned dumping in the context of the WTO and domestic AD laws.
5. Section 2 of the *Sherman Act.*
6. For example, China's *Law against Unfair Competition* (Article 11) and *Price Law* (Article 14).

defined under competition laws.[1] Nonetheless, the position requirement, like the intent test, is absent from AD laws.

In 2006, the European Commission published its *Green Paper on Trade Defence Instruments*, in which it argued that 'the economic justification for antidumping measures derives chiefly from the fact that international markets are imperfectly competitive – there is no international competition authority to regulate anti-competitive behaviour between countries' (2006b:4). This sounds appealing but cannot survive careful scrutiny, because were there an international competition legal system in place, modelled on either US or EC competition laws, injurious dumping *per se*, as defined under AD laws, would not be prohibited. Treating foreign dumped products differently from domestic ones under the *WTO AD Agreement* and national AD laws is actually inconsistent with the WTO national treatment principle (GATT 1994 Article III) and more generally the right to be treated equally before the law at domestic level.

Third, in a series of documents recently tabled at the WTO, the US argues that AD rules are not intended as a remedy for predatory pricing or any other private anti-competitive practices with which competition laws are concerned. It then asserts that dumping is *typically* the result of government policies in the dumping exporter's home market, which provide artificial advantages to the benefiting exporter.[2] Similarly, the European Commission, in its *Green Paper* (2006b:4), attributes dumping to state interference in exporters' home markets such as artificially low raw material and energy prices set by the government.

Economically, two measures can create a home sanctuary market for a particular industry: high import tariffs at the border and subsidies within the country. However, the tariff-created home sanctuary market problem, if any, can be easily addressed by incorporating an 'import duties on like products comparison clause' into AD laws, but the US and the EC have never proposed this. In addition, significantly declining duty levels among all WTO members after the Uruguay Round casts further doubt on the creditability of the tariff account. On the other hand, the subsidy argument of the US and the EC is even less analytically grounded. It is widely accepted by economists that subsidies granted by government to particular industrial sectors distort the operation of the market economy of free trade and competition, and thus should be prohibited (Finger and Zlate 2005; Rowley *et al.* 1995:65–66; Samuelson and Nordhaus 1998:ch. 2). Nevertheless, WTO already has Article VI of the *GATT 1994* and the *Agreement on Subsidies and Countervailing Measures* in place to regulate trade-distorting subsidies. To justify AD by condemning government subsidies is simply adopting a red herring strategy.

1. Article 18 of the *Anti-Trust Law of China* and Section 7 of the *Competition Act 1998 of South Africa.*
2 WTO: WT/WGTCP/W/88, (1998:2); TN/RL/W/27 (2002:4); and TN/RL/W/35 (2003).

The fourth anti-competitive characteristic of AD is its tolerance and even encouragement of price fixing between collusive companies, which is completely prohibited under competition laws. Large percentages of AD cases are withdrawn before the imposition of final AD duties, terminating in a price-undertaking agreement between exporters and investigating authorities or domestic claimants to raise prices of the allegedly dumped products (Stegemann 1990; DeVault 1990; Prusa 1992).[1] Not surprisingly, such agreements would logically be less harmful than import duties to the interests of exporters: sometimes the increased price may even offset the profit loss resulting from the decreased volume of exports. However, they perfectly meet the standard of price fixing under competition laws, with the investigating authorities actually working as a broker, usually biased towards the complaining parties (Baldwin and Moore 1991). We do not see any reason for the preferential treatment of foreign-related price fixing over price fixing by domestic companies, even though the former is in fact exempt from competition laws in all countries which have an AD law in place.[2]

Finally, while there can be little doubt that the spirit of competition laws is that small firms deserve special government intervention to be protected from the abuse of market power by big firms, AD laws appear to have been designed in the reverse direction.

Legally, to be a target of an AD investigation, a foreign producer can be very small in terms of its imports and thus market share – no less than 3 per cent – in the importing country. Furthermore, if there are several producers from different countries in a dumping case, even if the share of each of them is less than 3 per cent, they cannot escape the threat of AD, as long as those foreign producers collectively account for no less than 7 per cent of total imports of the like product in the importing country.[3] By contrast, to apply for AD protection, domestic producers must hold at least a 25 per cent production share in their own country.[4] Even though there is no legal requirement regarding the share of individual producers who lodge complaints, in practice diffused small producers such as individual farmers can hardly meet the production share requirement (the industry standing test). Protecting domestic producers who account for at least a 25 per cent production share from competition from foreign producers with an import share of 3 or even less per cent can, by whatever standard, hardly promote competition and economic growth.

Table I shows that the sectoral distribution of AD initiations by all WTO members from 1995 to 2007 varied considerably. Of all AD initiations, 47 per cent were concentrated in chemicals (sector VI) and metals (sector XV), despite the relatively small import share of these two sectors. One explanation for the unevenness in distri-

1. This is allowed under the Article 8 of the *WTO AD Agreement.*
2. Such a preferential arrangement is not inconsistent with WTO law, which does not prohibit positive discriminatory treatment of imported products.
3. Article 5.8 of the *WTO AD Agreement.*
4. Article 5.4 of the *WTO AD Agreement.*

bution is that the relatively high standardisation of products in certain sectors makes determinations on like products easier in AD applications and investigations and thus leads to more AD cases. However, a less obvious characteristic shared by these sectors, as opposed to sectors such as agriculture and textiles and clothing, is their oligopolistic market structures, i.e., most output and market share is concentrated among a handful of big producers, which results in low, if any, coordination costs for them to pass the industry standing test (25 per cent) for AD applications. Ironically, domestic sectors filing most dumping and injury complaints are quite often those which already enjoy substantial government support and rapid expansion in both

Table I: Harmonised System Sectoral Distribution of AD Initiations by all WTO Members, China and South Africa (1995–2007)

		Totals and %	I	II	III	IV	V	VI	VII	IX	X	XI	XII	XIII	XV	XVI	XVII	XVIII	XX
WTO Members	Top 7 Sectors of AD Initiations	3,220						655	420		161	232		110	876	290			
	% of Total Initiations	100						20	13		5	7		3	27	9			
China	Initiations	148	0	0	0	1	4	89	26	0	12	4	0	0	8	4	0	0	0
	% of Total Initiations*	100					3	60	18		8	3			5	3			
South Africa	Initiations	205	2	2	2	0	0	28	36	2	17	10	1	26	53	14	2	8	1
	% of Total Initiations*	100						14	18		8	5		13	26	7			

VI Products of the Chemical or Allied Industries.

VII Plastics and Articles Thereof; Rubber and Articles Thereof.

X Pulp of wood or of other fibrous cellulosic material; recovered (waste and scrap) paper or paperboard; paper and paperboard and articles thereof.

XI Textiles and textile articles.

XIII Articles of Stone; Plaster; Cement; Asbestos; Mica or Similar Materials; Ceramic Products; Glass and Glassware.

XV Base Metals and Articles of Base Metals.

XVI Machinery and mechanical appliances; electrical equipment; parts thereof; sound recorders and reproducers, television image and sound recorders and reproducers, and parts and accessories of such articles.

* Only percentages of AD initiations in the top seven sectors are presented.

Note: AD initiations are calculated using the WTO per country per product methodology.

Source: WTO Statistics on Anti-Dumping.

domestic and international markets, as is the case in the chemical industries of China and South Africa.[1]

Taking as an example China and South Africa, where the top seven national AD sectors are almost identical to those of the world, it is found in Table II that of the 36 AD investigations (cases) launched by China in the past six years, twenty-one (58 per cent) involved no more than two petitioners, who collectively held at least a 25 per cent domestic production share. The case of South Africa during the same period is even more striking – a single producer exceeded the industry standing test in 70 per cent of cases and most of them were the sole manufacturer of related products.[2] On the other hand, the number of target countries is two or more in 89 per cent cases launched by China. In short, AD in both China and South Africa has been largely used to protect big and concentrated domestic producers from competition from their much more diffused foreign rivals, an absurd situation from the perspective of competition laws. Although these two countries have a self-initiation provision in their AD laws, which allows AD authorities to initiate an investigation *sua sponte* in

Table II: Concentration of Applicants and Target Countries of AD Investigations by China and South Africa (2002–07)

China: 36 Cases; 117 AD Initiations					**South Africa:** 30 Cases; 48 AD Initiations				
Domestic Petitioner(s)	**Cases**	**% of Total Cases**	**Initi-ations**	**% of Total Initiations**	**Domestic Petitioner(s)**	**Cases**	**% of Total Cases**	**Initi-ations**	**% of Total Initiations**
1	14	39	30	26	1	21	70	29	60
2	7	19	30	26	2	6	20	9	19
3	6	17	29	25	3	1	3	1	2
≥4	9	15	28	24	≥4	1	3	1	2
					n/a	1	3	8	17
Target Countries	**Cases**	**% of Total Cases**			**Target Countries**	**Cases**	**% of Total Cases**		
1	4	11			1	18	69		
≥2	32*	89			≥2	12	40		

* Including one case against EC as a whole.
Note: One case may include more than one initiation.
Source: MOFCOM of China and ITAC of South Africa.

1. Business Monitor International (2008a; 2008b).
2. This is consistent with an analysis by Holden (2002), which shows that 69 per cent of the South African AD applicants from 1991 to 1998 were made by the sole manufacturer of the product in question.

cases, *inter alia*, where producers in certain sectors are too diffused and poorly organised to effectively launch an AD complaint,[1] this power has never been exercised.

In conclusion, AD, while ostensibly aiming at offsetting 'unfair' trade practices, actually distorts the law of comparative advantage and competition at both national and international levels by protecting inefficient but concentrated domestic industries from competition from their efficient and relatively diffused foreign rivals.

2.2 AD: Misunderstanding, Ignorance and Indifference

The comparative advantage principle of free trade, while widely accepted as standard economic theory, is not readily accessible to ordinary people. What makes the situation worse is that, unlike classic simple and clear work by Ricardo (1821), F. Bastiat ([1845] and Mill ([1848], today's researchers, from both liberal and conservative camps, adopt convoluted econometric methodologies to develop their arguments (Gilpin 2000:18). These are hardly comprehensible to non-specialists. In the case of AD, a trade protectionist policy that is highly technical and carries an emotive rhetorical claim to address 'unfair foreign' competition by protecting 'national' industries, is likely to distract the attention of the general public away from the underlying reality.

In addition, while trade protectionist policies, including AD, significantly undermine the benefits of the law of comparative advantage and free competition and thus result in huge cost to the economy as a whole, individual consumers are only slightly affected by it, because losses are diffused and small, as, conversely are the benefits of free trade to them (Destler 2005:ch. 1; Downs 1957; Olson 1965; Samuelson and Nordhaus 1998:ch. 35). Consequently, they have no great incentive to figure out the rationale for a particular trade policy and to influence the policy-making process by voting or other political action, for that could cost most of them more than the benefit any such policy could generate.

2.2.1 Collaboration between Special Interest Groups and Decision Makers

Information-, Incentive-, and Political Influence-Advantages of AD Protection-Seekers

Trade and competition, even while benefiting society as a whole, do not necessarily help everybody at the same time and to the same extent. Free international trade results in intense competition on a global scale and competition leads to winners and losers, at least in the short run. 'No industry willingly dies; no region gladly undergoes conversion to new industries' (Samuelson and Nordhaus 1998:705). These temporary losers, even though they might be aware they will also benefit from free competition in the long run, often feel they are being singled out to carry the burden of progress (*ibid.*), and constitute an ever-present force that could overthrow

1. Article 18 of the AD Regulation 2002 of China and Section 3 of the AD Regulations 2003 of South Africa.

or at least significantly disrupt the market system of trade and competition (Gilpin 2000:3; Mueller 1991:330; Smith [1776] 1947:book II, ch.iv).

Compared with the lay public, specific industries seeking protection enjoy a number of advantages in affecting public decision making. First, while the potential benefits of free trade for an economy are much greater than the costs caused by the transition or even collapse of certain industries and firms under the pressure of foreign competition, the former are, as mentioned above, diffused and modest for each individual, while the latter are concentrated on specific industries or a relatively small number of firms (Destler 2005:ch.1; Lamb 2006). The greater the potential losses from free trade and competition, the greater the incentives for domestic industry to seek protection (Baldwin 1984; Mueller 1991:241; Schattschneider 1935:285).

In addition, industries competing with imports, like other special groups, are usually well organised and funded, due partly to their small size relative to consumers and partly to the common interests they share (Bhagwati 1989; Gilpin 2000:99; Stigler 1971, 1975; Samuelson and Nordhaus1998:ch.17). As long as some of them command expertise in the rationale for trade and can develop specious anti-trade arguments, the rest will simply follow in their own interest. By contrast, diffused consumers, often poorly informed about trade theories, generally do not loyally embrace economists' pro-trade ideas, but are frequently susceptible to popular misconceptions (Gilpin 2000:18). The relative information cost for special groups is much less than for the lay public.

Finally, the effective organisation of import-competing industries also precludes the free-riding problem that is rampant in the consumers' camp. Thus, the former may have great political weight far beyond the numerical size of their membership, while the weight of consumers' votes and other political influence may be close to zero due to their low participation in trade-related political actions and the internal counteractions between pro-trade members and those deluded by anti-trade and competition fallacies. The high expectation of being able to influence the outcomes of policy-making strengthens the incentive of protection seekers to invest time and money in political campaigns (Bhagwati 1989; Gilpin 2000:99; Samuelson and Nordhaus1998:ch.17; Tullock 1974:380, 1996).

Decision Makers in Favour of Protection Seekers

Between the lay public and special interest groups is the government. Traditionally, governments, as opposed to the market, which is made up of self-interested private agents, are thought to work for something called the public interest. However, this wisdom has been increasingly challenged by commentators from the school of public choice (in particular Buchanan and Tullock). They, as Samuelson and Norhaus note (1998:ch.17), contend that the game of politics, like the game of markets, must match people's demands for collective goods with the economy's capacity to supply them. The major difference lies in the fact that the central players in politics

– politicians – are primarily concerned with *winning political support*, while the major market players – business firms – aim at *earning profits*.

Unsurprisingly, decision makers, by and large tend to favour well organised protectionist interest groups, who have greater political weight (Gilpin 2000:99), unless government interventions in free trade have become so pervasive and intrusive as to render even the average cost to individual consumers intolerable. In such a situation, the general public will become one of great incentives for removing these protections and can prevail over special interest groups in influencing policy makers, as happened during the period leading to the removal of the notorious *Smoot-Hawley Tariff Act of 1930*.[1]

Tariffs and quotas have played a major role in protecting domestic interest groups from foreign competition in human history, but their role is much more limited today. The average tariff rates have dramatically declined and most import quotas are basically prohibited, thanks to the role of the GATT/WTO system in achieving collaboration on trade liberalisation among countries in the context of accelerating economic globalisation. Unsurprisingly, protection seekers must find new weapons. AD is a legitimate weapon under WTO law. It is highly technical and complex for the public, replete with numerous loopholes that leave much room for decision makers to manipulate proceedings and results, but grounded in the specious argument of addressing unfair foreign competition. Consequently, there is no reason for governments pursuing political support to refuse to use the low profile AD instrument, which caters to special interest groups without arousing the attention of the general public.

In summary, the analysis above clearly shows that AD has little to do with fairness or with level playing fields. AD trade protection enjoys broad political support merely because its convoluted technical complexities prevent all but a few insiders and experts from understanding the reality that underlies the rhetoric. Thus inefficient but well-organised domestic producers may safely utilise it in protecting themselves from foreign competition, at times in collusion with exporters and with the national AD authorities as a broker. Despite the absence of an international competition authority, the alleged goals of AD may be achieved perfectly by national competition laws. If there is a need of any change in the AD instrument, the best option is undoubtedly *complete removal.*

1. The Act set an average duty at the highest level in US history, resulted in quick and intense retaliation by Europeans (Jones 1934:1; Stokes and Choate 2001), and helped drag the US economy into the Great Depression (Destler 2000:ch.1; Mises 1944:ch.3).

3. Harnessing Anti-Dumping: a good Governance Approach

The previous section concluded that complete removal is the best option for AD reform. Unfortunately, this option, no matter how economically convincing, is not politically practicable. The elimination or even material reform of the AD instrument at the WTO has been ruled out in the Doha Ministerial Declaration (2001: para.28), and the latest version of the Draft Chair Texts of the AD Agreement presented by the WTO Negotiating Group on Rules reflects little will, if any, to impose substantially stricter disciplines on AD.[1] Therefore, it appears that efforts to improve AD must be made at the national level and focus on procedural issues. This section proposes promoting the quality of national authorities' AD decision-making processes from the perspective of good governance as the second best option for reforming AD. It argues that poor governance in AD decision formulation may contribute to the arbitrary and proliferating use of AD by developing countries.

3.1 Good Governance in AD Decision Making

Public governance concentrates on the quality of the decision-making process and good governance is considered as being essential to promoting the quality of decision outcomes (Buchanan 1980; Krueger 1974:291; World Bank 1992, 1998, 2000; OECD 1997, 2002).

In the case of AD, process- rather than substance-focused good governance has little to do with the justifications for the alleged economic and social goals of AD, but helps to enhance the quality of the investigation process and thus of final outcomes – determinations on the existence of dumping and, if affirmative, the imposition of AD measures. A variety of organisations have developed a plethora of criteria for or indicators of good governance in various public sectors.[2] For reasons of space, three of them are seen as being of particular importance to AD, namely transparency, stakeholder participation and the rule of law.

Transparency is the prerequisite for and the starting point of good governance (European Commission 2006a; OECD 2005; Lloyd et al. 2007; ODI 2006; UNDP 1999; UNESCAP 2007). The process of policy-making is laid bare to the public at large, thereby reducing misunderstanding and increasing public trust. Transparency makes outside advice and scrutiny possible, which will undoubtedly improve the quality of decision outcomes and the accountability of the actors. Transparency is also closely linked to the fundamental human right to freedom of information, which

1. WTO: TN/RL/W/213, 30 Nov 2007. The draft agreement even relaxes rather than tightens the obligations of the AD investigating authorities in some regards. For example, the 'zeroing' dumping margin calculation methodology, which has been repeatedly condemned by the WTO Dispute Settlement Body (see e.g., the *Appellate Body Report on EC-Bed Linen (Article 21.5–India)*, WT/DS141/AB/R, 2001), is allowed under certain conditions under the draft.
2. For a systematic survey of good governance indicators, see UNDP (2007).

was regarded as 'the touch-stone of all the freedoms to which the United Nations is consecrated' at the very first session of the UN General Assembly.[1] The WTO AD Agreement requires all members to refer their national AD laws to the appropriate committee for scrutiny by other members, but does not provide a high standard of transparency for other information, including details of the reasoning behind determinations by national investigating authorities, thus leaving individual countries with considerable leeway. Given the technical complexity of AD, transparency here is of more significance than in many other public decision-making sectors.

Stakeholder participation is at the core of democracy and the legitimacy of public governance. Moreover, wide participation is likely to enhance the quality of the end results of policy-making, as a result of the intellectual competition by various stakeholders from different standpoints. Given appropriate opportunities to be heard and to influence the decision-making process, participants will be more willing to accept final decisions and this can reduce obstacles to their implementation. The AD decision-making process is actually dominated by the bargaining or collusion between domestic import-competing industries and foreign dumpers with the AD investigating authorities as a broker in the middle. Other stakeholders, including consumers and downstream users of the target imported product, are hardly able to have input due in part to their inferior financial and organisational position. Wide and balanced participation by stakeholders is essential to the governance quality of AD.

The principle of rule of law entails clear and predictable legal provisions and an objective, reliable and independent judiciary. More important is the respect for, confidence in and compliance with published laws by stakeholders, in particular the government itself (Freedom House 2007; OECD 2005; UNDP 1999; UNESCAP 2007; Kaufmann et al. 2008). AD laws and practices are characterised by excessive discretionary power for the importing countries' authorities to manipulate the results of investigations and thus give rise to a non-trivial element of unpredictability. AD decision-formulation is in urgent need of stricter and clearer discipline in respect of the powers and obligations of the administrative authorities and an effective judicial remedy for violations of this discipline.

3.2 The Prolific Use of AD by Emerging Economies and the Low Quality of Governance

Given the significant decline in traditional trade barriers, it is not surprising that AD is playing an increasingly important role in trade protection, that more AD laws are adopted and that more investigations are initiated and measures imposed.

1. UN General Assembly, *Resolution 50(I)*, 1946.

Table III: Shares of Top Ten AD Users in World Merchandise Imports and inWTO AD Initiations (1998–2007)

		1998	1999	2000	2001	2002	2003	2004	2005	2006	2007	Totals and %
World	Total Imports (US$ bn)	5,682	5,920	6,725	6,482	6,742	7,859	9,559	10,842	12,413	13,940	86,164
	AD Initiations by WTO Members	257	361*	290	366	312	232	214	200	201	159	2592*
Argentina	Imports (US$ bn)	31	26	25	20	9	14	22	29	34	45	255
	% of World Imports	0.55	0.44	0.37	0.31	0.14	0.18	0.23	0.27	0.27	0.32	**0.30**
	AD Initiations	8	23	43	27	14	1	12	12	11	8	159
	% of AD Initiations by WTO Members	3.11	6.37	14.83	7.34	4.49	0.43	5.61	6.00	5.47	5.03	**6.13**
India	Imports (US$ bn)	43	47	52	50	57	73	100	139	175	217	953
	% of World Imports	0.76	0.79	0.77	0.77	0.85	0.93	1.05	1.28	1.41	1.56	**1.11**
	AD Initiations	28	64	41	79	81	46	21	28	34	46	468
	% of AD Initiations by WTO Members	10.89	17.73	14.14	21.58	25.96	19.83	9.81	14.00	16.92	28.93	18.06
South Africa	Imports (US$ bn)	29	27	30	28	29	40	53	62	77	91	466
	% of World Imports	0.51	0.46	0.45	0.43	0.43	0.51	0.55	0.57	0.62	0.65	**0.54**
	AD Initiations	41	16	21	6	4	8	6	23	3	5	133
	% of AD Initiations by WTO Members	15.95	4.43	7.24	1.64	1.28	3.45	2.80	11.50	1.49	3.14	**5.13**
Brazil	Imports (US$ bn)	61	52	59	59	50	51	66	78	96	127	699
	% of World Imports	1.07	0.88	0.88	0.91	0.74	0.65	0.69	0.72	0.77	0.91	**0.81**
	AD Initiations	18	16	11	17	8	4	8	6	12	13	113
	% of AD Initiations by WTO Members	7.00	4.43	3.79	4.64	2.56	1.72	3.73	3.00	5.97	8.18	4.36
Mexico	Imports (US$ bn)	131	146	183	176	177	178	207	232	268	297	1,995
	% of World Imports	2.31	2.47	2.72	2.72	2.63	2.26	2.17	2.14	2.16	2.13	**2.32**
	AD Initiations	12	11	6	6	10	14	6	6	6	3	80
	% of AD Initiations by WTO Members	7.64	3.05	2.07	1.64	3.21	6.03	2.80	3.00	3.00	1.89	**3.07**

		1998	1999	2000	2001	2002	2003	2004	2005	2006	2007	Totals and %
China	Imports (US$ bn)	140	166	225	244	295	413	561	660	791	956	4,451
	% of World Imports	2.46	2.80	3.35	3.76	4.38	5.27	5.87	6.09	6.37	6.86	**5.17**
	AD Initiations	0	7*	6	14	30	22	27	24	11	4	145
	% of AD Initiations by WTO Members	0	1.94	2.07	3.83	9.62	9.48	12.62	12.00	5.47	2.41	**5.59**
Australia	Imports (US$ bn)	75	83	89	90	86	104	120	139	161	165	1,112
	% of World Imports	1.32	1.40	1.32	1.39	1.28	1.32	1.26	1.28	1.30	1.18	**1.30**
	AD Initiations	13	24	15	23	16	8	9	7	10	2	127
	% of AD Initiations by WTO Members	5.06	6.65	5.17	6.28	5.13	3.45	4.21	3.50	4.98	1.26	**4.90**
Canada	Imports (US$ bn)	206	220	245	227	227	245	280	321	358	390	2,719
	% of World Imports	3.63	3.72	3.64	3.50	3.37	3.12	2.93	2.96	2.88	2.80	**3.16**
	AD Initiations	8	18	21	25	5	15	11	1	7	1	112
	% of AD Initiations by WTO Members	3.11	5.00	7.24	6.83	1.60	6.47	5.14	0.50	3.48	0.63	**4.32**
US	Imports (US$ bn)	944	1,059	1,259	1,179	1,200	1,303	1,526	1,735	1,919	2,017	14,141
	% of World Imports	16.61	17.89	18.72	18.19	17.80	16.58	15.96	16.00	15.46	14.47	**16.41**
	AD Initiations	36	47	47	75	35	37	26	12	7	29	351
	% of AD Initiations by WTO Members	14.01	13.02	16.21	20.49	11.22	15.95	12.15	6.00	3.48	18.24	13.54
EC	Imports (US$ bn)	796	831	920	881	891	1,065	1,280	1,461	1,697	1,949	11,771
	% of World Imports	14.01	14.04	13.68	13.59	13.22	13.55	13.91	13.48	13.67	13.98	**13.66**
	AD Initiations	22	65	32	28	20	7	30	25	35	9	273
	% of AD Initiations by WTO Members	8.56	18.01	11.03	7.65	6.41	3.02	14.02	12.50	17.41	5.66	10.53

* China acceded to the WTO in 2001. Therefore, the WTO data on AD do not include the seven initiations in 1999 by China, since China was not obliged to report its AD data to the WTO at that time. These initiations, however, are included here.

Note: In order to reveal these countries' AD initiation frequency relative to their share in world imports, it would be better to compare their share of AD initiations in all countries of the world, rather than those with only WTO members, with their share in world imports. However, given the negligible share of non-WTO countries in AD initiations, the error cannot be significant.

Source: AD initiations: WTO Statistics on Anti-Dumping; WTO Members' *Semi-Annual Reports* to Commit tee on Anti-Dumping Practices and Government Gazette by Bureau of Fair Trade, Ministry of Commerce of China; Imports: WTO *International Trade Statistics 2007* and *World Trade 2007, Prospects for 2008*; Others: Author's calculation.

Yet what deserves particular attention is the fact that developing countries, as new users, resort to AD much more widely than before, even exceeding the use of AD by industrial countries. According to Niels and Kate's calculation (2006: 619), the four traditional AD users – the US, the EC, Canada and Australia – accounted for around 90 per cent of all AD cases between 1969 and 1993. However, since 1993, developing countries have initiated more AD investigation than the four traditional users combined. This led to a reduction in the traditional users' share to 37% in 1998–2001.

Table III presents the data with respect to AD initiation and import amounts and shares of the top ten AD users in the past decade. Six developing countries – new users – initiated 1,098 AD investigations (per product per country), accounting for 42.4 per cent of all initiations by WTO members, while their collective share of world imports is only 10.2 per cent. However, even though the four traditional users – industrial countries – launched 863 AD initiations, their AD initiation share (33.3 per cent) and import share (34.5 per cent) are basically compatible. The individual countries from both camps are arranged in descending order by their ratio of AD share to import share. It is found that the ratios of all new users are above 1.0. For example, South Africa has only a 0.54 per cent share of world imports but accounts for 5.13 per cent of all AD initiations by WTO members. In the cases of Argentina and India, the respective ratios are astounding 20.4 and 16.4. Nonetheless, half the traditional users, the US and the EC, enjoy a ratio less than 1.0, reflecting a low intensity of AD initiations relative to their import share. Because these emerging countries' tariff rates already are considerably higher than those of industrial countries, other things being constant, new AD users' economies are indeed much less open.[1]

A large body of literature has explained: i) why, because of declining traditional trade barriers, there has been an increase in the adoption of AD laws and the use of AD over the past two decades and ii) why developing countries now account for a larger share in the adoption of AD laws and the use of AD (because most developed countries already had AD laws in place two decades ago and many new AD investigations were launched by developing countries for purposes of retaliation or trade protection) (Lindsey and Ikenson 2003; Moore and Zanardi 2006; Vandenbussche and Zanardi 2008; Wooton and Zanardi 2002:3). However, nobody convincingly answers the question raised by Table III: while both emerging economies and industrial countries confront the substantive defects of the AD instrument alike, since all are equally subject to the *WTO AD Agreement*, why is it that producers in developing countries are able, for whatever purpose, to initiate such a huge number of AD cases *relative to their countries' small imports*?

1. Calculation by Messerlin (1994), based on the volume of imports affected by AD duties, rather than the number of AD initiations, also shows a much higher share of imports are under AD duties in developing countries.

This section, by examining the quality of developing countries' AD decision-formulation process against the three criteria of good governance noted above, suggests that poor public governance in these emerging economies allows domestic protection-seekers to exploit the substantive defects in the AD instrument to the largest extent possible and thus gives rise to the arbitrary and prolific use of AD. They do so by exploiting the weakness in the domestic regulatory system as well as weak enforcement capacity of the national authorities. This has particularly been the case with the youngest and the oldest AD users – China and South Africa. These two countries, due respectively to, inter alia, the socialist economic system and the apartheid policy, were largely isolated from the international community and global economy for decades. International trade liberalisation is of particular importance to them.

3.2.1 AD Decision Making in China

Three decades ago, China launched its ambitious market-oriented economic reform and began opening up to international trade and foreign investment. In undertaking the transition from a centrally planned economy to a market oriented system, China developed a strong private sector, significantly reduced government intervention in economic activities and grew into the world's third largest economy in terms of nominal GDP.

China enacted its *Foreign Trade Law* in 1994, Article 30 of which sets out the principles of AD. This general provision was elaborated in the *Anti-dumping and Anti-Subsidy Regulation* modelled on related WTO agreements in 1997, and the first AD investigation was initiated a few months later. Immediately after its accession to the WTO in December 2001, China's separate *Anti-dumping Regulation* and *Anti-subsidy Regulation* came into force.

Two agencies in the Ministry of Commerce (MOFCOM) are currently in charge of AD investigations and determinations on dumping and injury: the Bureau of Fair Trade for Imports and Exports (BOFT) is responsible for the investigation process and determining the existence of dumping, and the Investigation Bureau of Industry Injury (BOII) investigates and determines injury, if any, caused to industry. The two are jointly in charge of determining the causal link between dumping and injury. Provisional and definitive AD measures are decided by the Tariff Commission of the State Council upon the recommendation of MOFCOM in the case of AD duty, and by MOFCOM if the measure is in the form of a bond or cash deposit.

Transparency

Since its economic reform, especially after WTO accession, China has endeavoured to improve transparency in its public governance (OECD 2005; WTO 2006:ch.2). While acknowledging that there have been significant improvements, the WTO and some of China's trading partners appear to expect more to be done. They warn that the current relatively low transparency in trade administration could still undermine China's public accountability and thus governance (USTR: 2008; WTO 2008:ch.2).

In the case of AD, China used to follow strictly the information disclosure requirements of the *WTO AD Agreement*, which is, however, a minimum standard. This has led to much criticism by researchers and practitioners. They argue that interested parties do not have sufficient access to information to restore the calculation of dumping margins due to confidentiality protection orders; that non-confidential filings and government reports are generally useless; and that the detailed decision-making procedure in MOFCOM is inaccessible to the public (Yu 2005:98–99). In August 2006, MOFCOM promulgated its *Rules on Information Access and Information Disclosure in Industry Injury Investigations (Information Rules)*, 'for the purposes of ensuring the openness, fairness and impartiality in the investigations of industry injury and safeguarding the legitimate rights and interests of the interested parties'.[1] There are basically four facets to the efforts to enhance transparency in AD.

First, under the *AD Regulation*, MOFCOM enjoys unlimited de jure discretion in determining the confidentiality of information requested by interested parties.[2] However, the *Information Rules* provide a relatively clear definition of 'confidential information' based on Article 6.5 of the *WTO AD Agreement*, i.e., any information that cannot be publicly obtained, and which, if disclosed, would confer a significant competitive advantage on a competitor or have a significantly adverse effect upon a person supplying the information. Such information is treated as confidential by MOFCOM.[3]

Second, the *Information Rules* provide detailed procedures based on Article 6.5.1 and 6.5.2 of the *WTO AD Agreement* in determining the confidentiality of information.[4] Interested parties are required to indicate in writing the reasons for confidentiality, and simultaneously furnish a public text or non-confidential summary that will contain *sufficient detail* to permit a reasonable understanding of the *substance* of the information submitted in confidence. 'In exceptional circumstances' interested parties may be exempt from this requirement by providing only 'a statement of the reasons why public text or non-confidential summaries are not possible'. However, no criteria for determining such exceptional situations are provided and the only requirement is MOFCOM's approval. Thus, not insignificant scope exists for undermining the purposes of transparency and fairness in the *Information Rules* as a whole.

Third, MOFCOM needs to disclose the 'basic facts on which the definitive determination is based'[5] 'thirty days before definitive determination is made' in

1. Article 1.
2. Article 22.
3. Article 9.
4. Article 11.
5. Article 18.

non-particular circumstances.[1] This is probably the most transparency-enhancing measure in the *Information Rules*. Unfortunately, while this provision clearly and comprehensively defines the scope of 'basic facts',[2] it fails to provide any standard for the 'particular circumstances' that are exempt from the 'thirty day' requirement, again leaving ample discretion to the authorities.

Finally, the *Information Rules* regulate access to and disclosure of information only in the investigations into industry injury, rather than those into issues of dumping.[3] Rules related to disclosure of information related to determinations of dumping are provided in China's *Provisional Rules on Disclosure of Information in Anti-dumping Investigations 2002*. However, even though the *Provisional Rules* provide a detailed list of categories of information subject to disclosure, no information is required to be released before the preliminary determination. In addition, the *Provisional Rules* contain only 13 short articles covering two pages and lack detailed procedural guidance.

Compared to detailed substantive and procedural provisions in the US AD laws on access to information in AD investigations,[4] China's rules appear much less clear and practical. The authorities may, in many cases, simply issue their determinations without having to sufficiently elaborate the reasoning behind their determinations or the data on which they are based. All this may lead to easy manipulation by the authorities of the results of AD investigations in favour of domestic parties.

Stakeholder Participation

One key characteristic of AD is that it 'disenfranchises' (a term borrowed from Finger, Hall and Nelson 1982:454) one set of stakeholders, i.e., domestic users of the allegedly dumped products (either household consumers or downstream industrial users). AD laws, including those in the US, are explicitly intended to protect domestic producers from foreign competition. Thus, unsurprisingly, they deliberately ignore the interests of the opposite sets of stakeholders, both foreign exporters and domestic users. In this regard, China is no exception.

However, one point worth particular attention is the incorporation by China of a public interest clause in its *AD Regulation* in 2004. Matching provisions are currently absent in the *WTO AD Agreement* and US AD laws. First, only a price undertaking made by an exporter is acceptable and in the public interest and MOFCOM may decide to suspend or terminate the anti-dumping investigation without applying provisional anti-dumping measures or imposing anti-dumping duties.[5] Second,

1. Article 20.
2. Article 19.
3. Article 2.
4. See, Section 777 – access to information under the *Tariff Act of 1930*; Section 135(b) – prohibition on release of customer names under the *Customs and Trade Act of 1990*; 19 C.F.R. 351 and 354 of the *DOC Regulations*; 19 C.F.R. 201 and 207 of the *ITC Rules*; and Section A.4 – procedural rules for proceedings and Section C.4.a.(4) – public and proprietary records of *Statement of Administrative Action*.
5. Article 33.

if a final determination establishes the existence of dumping and injury caused by dumping to a domestic industry, an anti-dumping duty may be imposed, but imposition and collection of anti-dumping duties shall be in the public interest.[1] Legally, a public interest clause may function as a requirement that the AD authorities serve as the representatives of a broader interest, rather than focus exclusively on injury to domestic import-competing industries. If strictly and appropriately implemented, this provision can serve as an alternative, albeit imperfect, to direct participation by consumers and downstream industrial users, who are usually poorly organised in trade protection campaigns.

However, as noted above, AD is by definition designed to protect domestic import-competing industries and is, by nature, inconsistent with the wider interests of the society as a whole. This leads to an insurmountable dilemma, i.e., if a public interest clause is followed perfectly, there may have to be no AD at all. In addition, China's *AD Regulation* neither provides a clear definition of public interest nor contains detailed procedural requirements in the determination of it (e.g., whose and what information should be solicited and taken into account and in what manner), leaving almost unlimited discretion to the authorities. Since China's AD initiation in 1997, only seven of 48 cases have resulted in no definitive AD duties, due either to no material injury being found or to the withdrawal by complaining parties: public interest has never served as a reason for those negative AD decisions. In other words, there is little empirical evidence that China's authorities take the public interest clause seriously in AD decision making.

The Rule of Law

A requirement of the principle of rule of law is clear and predictable legal provisions. However, China's AD laws, being modelled on the *WTO AD Agreement,* appear to have inherited the original sins in this agreement, namely ample leeway for manipulation and vague language. What makes the situation worse is China's explicit retaliation clause. China has been at the top of the list of AD target countries for at least 16 years. From 1995 to 2007, WTO members initiated 597 AD investigations against and imposed 423 definitive AD measures on China's exports, numbers several times higher than those of the silver medallist.[2] Many researchers regard retaliation as a possible explanation for the proliferation of AD laws and AD cases (Blonigen and Bown 2003; Bagwell and Staiger 1999, 2002; Feinberg and Reynolds 2006; Prusa and Skeath 2002; Vandenbussche and Zanardi 2008). China, in this regard, offers a primary *de jure* example.

Article 56 of China's *AD Regulation* provides that 'where a country (region) discriminatorily imposes anti-dumping or countervailing measures on the exports from China, China may, on the basis of the actual situations, take corresponding

1. Article 37.
2. WTO, Statistics on Anti-dumping, http://www.wto.org/english/tratop_e/adp_e/adp_e.htm.

measures against such country (region)'. Similar even more explicit and less diplomatic provisions are found in China's *Foreign Trade Law*[1] and the *AD Regulation* before the amendment in 2004.[2] In 2003, China explained at the WTO, in response to inquiries by other countries, that 'corresponding measures' refers to 'the measures China is entitled to take after recourse to the dispute settlement procedures pursuant to the Anti-Dumping Agreement if the counterpart country is a WTO Member'.[3] However, as it happened this US-style definition[4] was not incorporated into the current *AD Regulation* during its last amendment in 2004. So far, no AD investigations have been initiated based on this clause. However, given that WTO laws prohibit members from taking retaliatory measures against other members before the Dispute Settlement Body has addressed the complaint,[5] and that this unilateral retaliatory clause provides great discretionary power for retaliation to MOFCOM, Article 56 of the *AD Regulation* appears inconsistent with the spirit of the principle of the rule of law.

In addition, because AD protection is dependent on administrative rather than judicial decisions, it tends to be vulnerable to political pressures (Nelson 2006:4). Consequently, external remedies independent of the executive branch are particularly necessary to ensure strict compliance by the administrative authorities with AD rules. In China, both the dumping and injury bureaus cooperate in AD investigations under the leadership of the head of MOFCOM. Thus, unlike the US, where the independent and quasi-judicial International Trade Commission (ITC) offers input into the review of injury information *prior to* initiation and then determines the existence of material injury from the alleged dumping, thereby serving as a check and balance in AD cases,[6] China's investigating authorities are more susceptible to political influence.

Effective post-AD review mechanisms may correct inappropriate administrative decisions and even help to deter the arbitrary exercise of public power by the competent authorities before a decision is made. Under China's general *Administrative Reconsideration Law 1999* and *Administrative Litigation Law 1989* and the specific *AD Regulation*, any interested party unsatisfied with decisions of the AD authorities may apply for administrative reconsideration or file a lawsuit in the people's court. In 2002, the Supreme People's Court, in its *Rules on Certain Issues Related to Appli-*

1. Article 7.
2. Article 40.
3. WTO: G/ADP/Q1/CHN/33, G/SCM/Q1/CHN/33, 24, October 2003, reply to Question 37.
4. The US law (e.g., Section 301 of the *Trade Act* of 1974) also allows trade retaliation for violations of WTO and other trade agreements by other countries, but such retaliation must be taken under the auspices of international law, e.g., the US Trade Representative will seek authority from the WTO's Dispute Settlement Body to suspend trade concessions previously granted to the foreign country.
5. Article 23 of the *WTO Understanding on Rules and Procedures Governing the Settlement of Disputes.*
6. At least 15 per cent of all cases filed since 1979 did not pass the preliminary injury test adopted by the International Trade Commission (Horlick 2005:170).

cation of Law in Hearings of Antidumping Administrative Case, specified procedures for the judicial review of AD cases and appointed the Intermediate People's Court in Beijing as the responsible review body. However, no judicial suit has been filed thus far against any AD decision made by MOFCOM. Apart from the low degree of independence enjoyed by China's judicial system within an undemocratic regime, there may be at least two other explanations for the reluctance by interested parties to sue, one institutional and the other technical.

In the US, the Court of International Trade is established to deal specifically with trade cases. China appoints common courts at the second lowest of four tiers to hear AD cases of high complexity against a ministry-level administrative agency. This tends to undermine the confidence of interested parties in both the judges' professional competence and the courts' authority.[1] Furthermore, practitioners complain that the Supreme Court's *Rules* does not grant competent courts sufficient power in examining AD cases and thus contribute to the reluctance of interested parties to sue (Yu 2005:99). Nonetheless, most, if not all, substantive and procedural issues in AD cases are subject to judicial review[2] and what is indeed lacking is a practical standard of review. The standard specified by the Supreme Court[3] is no less detailed than that provided by the US statute,[4] but the latter is accompanied by a set of well-developed judicial interpretations by the Court of International Trade over decades.[5] Consequently, interested parties and lawyers in the US do not have to face the high level of unpredictability that discourages their Chinese counterparts from initiating administrative litigation.

Two appeals have been made by exporters from the US and Japan respectively to MOFCOM for administrative reconsideration. MOFCOM's decision was reversed in the US case but upheld in the case of Japan. Detailed arguments were provided by MOFOCM for the maintenance of its decision in the latter case but no reason is available for the reversal of the original decision in the former.[6] The US Trade Representative (USTR), in its *National Trade Estimate Report on Foreign Trade Barriers 2008*, implies that the threat by the US to commence dispute settlement at the WTO was key in China's decision to repeal the definitive AD duty in the US case. Under

1. In a few instances of administrative litigation, ministry-level agencies lost. http://news3.xinhuanet.com/politics/2006–09/02/content_5038219.htm
2. Article 1.
3. Article 10.
4. Section 516A of the *Tariff Act* of 1930.
5. Even for minor disputes between the plaintiff and the AD authorities (both the International Trade Commission and the Department of Commerce), detailed legal guidance can be found in a variety of orders issued by the US courts (Rosen and Husisian 2006; Casson and Reynolds 2006).
6. MOFCOM published its Administrative Reconsideration Decision (2006) No. 67, on 5 Sep 2006. This provides a detailed explanation for the maintenance of its decision in the Japan case (Public Notice (2006) No. 18). However, even though in Public Notice (2006) No. 8 published on 13 Feb 2006, MOFCOM revoked its decision in the US case ((2006) No. 8) based on Administrative Reconsideration Decision (2006) No. 1, this Reconsideration Decision, unlike No. 67, is not provided on its website.

China's *Administrative Reconsideration Law 1999*, decisions made by province- and ministry-level authorities have to be reconsidered by the original authorities before complainants can appeal to the State Council led by the premier and the decision by the State Council is final and not subject to judicial review.[1] Unsurprisingly, reliance on the administrative reconsideration instrument to promote the rule of law in AD cases may not work as interested parties expect.

China's great achievement in improving public governance can by no means be dismissed. However, given the technical complexity and loose international regulation of AD, China may need to take further steps to cushion its government against national protectionist influence and to maintain its admirable economic development largely based on its free market- and free trade-oriented reforms.

3.2.2 AD Decision Formulation in South Africa

The South African economy is characterised by, *inter alia*, insufficient competition and high levels of concentration in the manufacturing sector, resulting from the decades of import substitution and apartheid policies (McCarthy 1988). Relying on one of the most complex and opaque tariff structures in the world (Belli *et al.* 1993) and high tariff barriers, domestic monopolies and duopolies, selected manufacturing industries were safely protected from foreign competition (Edwards and Lawrence 2008; McCarthy 2005). Since the 1990s, along with South Africa's great political democratisation and return to the international community, the South African trade regime has undergone considerable liberalisation, resulting in a simplified tariff structure and dramatically reduced tariff rates.[2] Tariff reduction is regarded as the main driving force behind the productivity growth experienced in South Africa during the 1990s (Harding and Rattso 2005; Jonsson and Subramanian 2001), but it also encouraged domestic protection-seekers to shift to non-tariff recourse, such as AD (Holden 2002). From 1995 to 2007, South Africa launched 205 AD initiations,[3] accounting for around 6 per cent of all AD initiations by WTO members, a rate 10 times higher than its share in world imports. Messerlin trade-weights South Africa's 108 AD definitive duties from 1995 to 2002 to reflect the average number of measures during this period per US$ 1,000 of 1997 imports and finds that South Africa's ratio of 1.81 is far higher than that of the second highest, namely India, at 1.28 (2004:107). There can be little doubt that AD has constituted a significant threat to South Africa's trade liberalisation and economic development.

South Africa is one of the oldest adopters of AD, with its first AD legislation promulgated in 1914.[4] AD investigations are currently conducted by the Trade Remedies Investigative Unit within the International Trade Administration Commission

1. Article 14.
2. The average rate was reduced from 27.5 per cent in 1990 to 8.2 per cent in 2006 (World Bank Trade and Production Database and WTO Trade Profiles).
3. Between 1914 and 1994, the total number of AD and anti-subsidy investigations was only 833 (Brink 2006:1).
4. S8(1) of the *Customs Tariff Act*, 26 of 1914.

(the Commission) in terms of the *International Trade Administration Act 2002* (the *ITA Act*), the *AD Regulations 2003* as second-tier legislation and the *WTO AD Agreement*.[1] The same team of staff investigates both dumping and injury (McCarthy 2005:58) and presents submissions to the Commission for its consideration. The Commission then recommends appropriate measures to the Minister of Trade and Industry (the Minister) for final decision.

Transparency

The South African AD system is basically consistent with the minimum requirements of the *WTO AD Agreement* with respect to notifications of AD laws and public notice of decisions by the AD authorities. However, few rules are provided to promote access to and disclosure of other information, resulting in low transparency throughout the whole investigation and decision-making process

In addition to the general *Promotion of Access to Information Act 2000*, only two sections of the *ITA Act* regulate information access and disclosure in AD cases, and provide no detailed substantive and procedural requirements. Section 33 categorises confidential information as confidential information by nature and other confidential information and requires information providers to present reasonable written support for their demands for confidentiality. Section 34 is supposed to provide guidance to the Commission in determining the confidentiality of information in question, but obviously fails. Section 34.1 (a) states that 'in the cases of information claimed to be confidential by nature, [the Commission must] determine whether the information satisfies the requirements of the definition of "information that is by nature confidential" set out in section 1(2)'. However, Section 1(2) does not itself define 'confidential information by nature' in any manner. This technical error was addressed one year later by the *AD Regulations*, Section 2.3 of which provides a list of information that is by nature confidential. Nonetheless, so far no corresponding modification has been made in the *ITA Act* itself. In the case of other information, no criterion of confidentiality is provided.[2] Moreover, Section 34.3 of the *ITA Act* simply states that the Commission must notify information providers of its determination of confidentiality, but does not require the Commission to provide any explanation of its decisions. Nevertheless, such explanation is regarded as obligatory for AD investigating authorities in many other countries and usually reasonable time will be granted to information providers to comment on the authorities' decisions.[3]

1. South Africa is part of the Southern African Customs Union (SACU) under the SACU Agreement, which came into operation on 15 July 2004. Because South Africa currently represents all SACU members in AD investigations, and all the other SACU economies are so small relative to South Africa's they are unlikely to meet the industry-standing test with respect to the SACU market (McCarthy 2005:60–1), this paper focuses on only South Africa's AD regime.
2. Section 34.1 (b).
3. See, e.g., Article 13 of China's *Rules on Information Access and Information Disclosure in Industry Injury Investigations* promulgated by MOFCOM.

In his recent paper (2005:148–9), Brink identifies seven symptoms of the lack of transparency in South Africa's AD system. These include: delayed access to dumping complaints; meaningless non-confidential questionnaire responses and other submissions; verification reports with little detail; no information disclosure of informal meetings between investigating officers and different interested parties; confidential Commission policy for applying AD rules; unknown decision-making process of the Commission; and Commission reports containing very little substantive and procedural information. Undoubtedly, these issues cannot be addressed without significant *de jure* improvement.

While the Commission is granted considerable discretionary power in determining the confidentiality of information, the *ITA Act* offers interested parties judicial remedies immediately afterwards. Interested parties who are not satisfied with the confidentiality-related decisions of the Commission may appeal to a High Court and then the Supreme Court of Appeal.[1] In practice, the judicial review body has clearly affirmed a standard of transparency higher than that held by the administration. For example, in *Rhone Poulenc v. Chairman of the Board*, the High Court ruled that:

> [U]nless all the information in possession of [ITAC] is supplied to the entity being investigated, the level of the investigation by [ITAC] never comes out into the open. The applicant had a right to be provided with all information in order to be put in a position where it would know all the ramifications of the case against it and in that way provided with the opportunity to meet the fifth respondent's case.[2]

Unfortunately, no *de jure* change reflecting the Court's views has yet been made to the South African system .

In summary, the South African AD system has few meaningful requirements for the Commission to ensure the transparency of its investigative and decision-making process. The judicial review mechanism may play a helpful role, but because of the limited number of judicial reviews initiated since the adoption of the *ITA Act* and the *AD Regulations*, the practical effect of judicial scrutiny in enhancing transparency remains to be seen.

Stakeholder Participation

As in many other countries, the AD laws of South Africa basically focus on the relationship between domestic producers as dumping complainants and AD applicants, and foreign exporters and domestic importers as defendants, and provide few if any opportunities for other stakeholders to participate directly in the process. There is also no explicit public interest clause of the sort found in many other countries' AD laws. Nevertheless, the *ITA Act* requires the Commission, in determining the imposition of AD duties, to investigate and evaluate matters that the Minister directs the Commission to consider or the Commission considers on its own initiative in

1. Sections 35, 36 and 37.
2. *Rhone Poulenc v. Chairman of the Board* (Case 6589/98 T), para. 26.

addition to the technical findings of dumping, injury and the link between them.[1] Given that the Minister is committed to promoting the economic growth of the country as a whole, it is not surprising that a broader interest – beyond that of the complainants – will be taken into account when considering recommendations by the Commission. Indeed, it appears that South African AD authorities have already placed considerable weight, maybe more in the future, on the interest of the society as a whole in AD cases, thereby serving as a proxy for representation by stakeholders excluded from direct participation in the AD determinations.

First, about half of AD initiations result in no definitive AD duty imposed in South Africa, a ratio similar to that in the US and Canada. In this regard, South Africa is one of the most reluctant developing country-AD users in the top ten, immediately following Brazil. It seems that one of the reasons for this is the concern for the interest of the economy as a whole. In the foreword of Commission's 2004/05 annual report, the Minister notes that the competitiveness problems in the country's manufacturing sector can be traced to the protectionist policies adopted decades ago. He also cautioned that the Commission 'needs to be wary of neo-protectionist tendencies in the form of anti-competitive, unfounded, or factitious anti-dumping and other trade remedy petitions from industry, the injudicious imposition of which would stifle our progress and precipitate non-competitiveness'. The Commission clearly accepted this guidance and indicated, in a later report (2007:21) that while AD duties can assist domestic industries in competing against low-priced imports, they also increase costs for domestic downstream users of these imports. This in turn affects the competitiveness of such users and national economic growth. Thus, the Comission notes, the AD instrument should not be used merely upon request of domestic industry. Even though it is not possible to measure the weight given *de facto* by South African authorities to public interest, owing to the limited access to the details of the authorities' decision making, parties complain the interests of domestic producers do not, *de jure,* receive the attention from the authorities that they deserve (Brink 2006).

In addition, it appears that South Africa, even though unwilling to scrub its AD laws, will further strengthen its *de facto* pro-public interest approach by legalising it. At the end of 2006, the Commission published extensive proposed amendments to the *AD Regulations.* Among these, Section 20.2 explicitly provides that the Minister, before a final decision on the imposition of AD duties, may instruct the Commission to consider the public interest and lists detailed, but non-exhaustive, factors that the Commission may consider in determining the potential impact of AD duties on the public interest. The interests of downstream users and consumers of the dumped imports, public health, public safety and even environmental protection are all aspects of public interest. Furthermore, the Commission may solicit information from any

1 Section 16(1).

source and in any manner it deems appropriate.[1] This indicates that a wide range of agents such as independent experts and consumer organisations may be able to participate directly in the determination process. Where the Commission determines that imposition or continuation of an AD duty is not in the public interest, it will specify in its recommendation to the Minister either that an AD duty not be imposed or be amended or be continued or that the level of reduction in the AD duty be determined after an investigation or review.[2]

It is unclear whether South Africa deliberately uses its pro-public interest approach as a counterweight to pressures for domestic protectionism, while preserving the AD instrument as a threat to be deployed against potential trade barriers to its exports by foreign countries and a bargaining chip in bilateral and multilateral trade negotiations. However, as an albeit imperfect alternative to wide and direct participation by all stakeholders, the pro-public interest approach may help reduce the use of AD and enhance the political acceptability of AD decisions. The insurmountable dilemma is, as noted above, that AD is by nature inconsistent with the interests of the society as a whole, so that if a public interest clause were to be followed perfectly, there may need to be no AD at all.

The Rule of Law

To meet the requirements of the principle of the rule of law, South Africa, like many other developing countries, including China, may have to make further efforts to improve its AD laws and the practices of its AD authorities.

First, within the Commission, the same team of investigators is responsible for both the determination of dumping and the subsequent injury analysis in specific AD cases (McCarthy 2005:58). Throughout the whole investigation process, there is no external scrutiny (like that by the US quasi-judicial ITC), and no internal checks and balances (such as between China's BOFT and BOII) exist in ensuring the principle of the rule of law.

In addition, the authorities' obligations are usually loosely and broadly defined *de jure* and are not strictly adhered to *de facto*. Taking time frames as an example, South African AD laws, as De Lange notes (2003), place few time limits on the Commission and most time limits apply to importers and exporters. One of the few exceptions is provided in Section 20 of the *AD Regulations*, whereby 'all investigations and reviews [by the Commission] shall be finalised within 18 months after initiation'. By comparison, Article 5.10 of the WTO *AD Agreement* requires that all AD investigations, *except in special circumstances*, be concluded within one year, and in no case more than 18 months. Given these discrepancies in time frames, doubts can easily be cast on the good faith of the South African government in fulfilling the letter and spirit of its commitment under the WTO law. What makes the situation

1. Section 20.2(c).
2. Section 22.2(d).

worse is the fact that the authorities can, and have in practice, completely disregarded some time limits, without having to give an explanation or take any responsibility.[1]

A third problem in guaranteeing the compliance of authorities with AD laws lies in South Africa's judicial review mechanism. Since the establishment of democracy in 1994 and the corresponding changes in the institutions and functions of the judiciary, the positive impact of court judgments, in particular those of the Constitutional Court, on a government limited by law has been widely acknowledged (Corder 2004:265). In the case of AD, decisions by executive authorities are subject to a two-tier judicial review process: first, on issues of law and fact before the High Court; and second, on appeal on issues of law before the Supreme Court of Appeal and on appeal on issues of a constitutional nature (e.g., freedom to information) before the Constitutional Court.[2] Nonetheless, since 1992 only a handful of AD decisions, preliminary or final, have been submitted for judicial review. Compare this with 61 reviews of AD decisions by the US Department of Commerce in 2005 alone by the US Court of International Trade and the US Court of Appeals for the Federal Circuit (Rosen and Husisian 2006). According to Brink, the situation in South Africa may not stem from the high quality and thus wide acceptance of administrative AD decisions, but from three other factors (2005:150). First, judicial reviews are usually time-consuming. In one case, the final judicial decision was rendered six and half years after the initiation of the review.[3] Second, the small volume of South African imports may not create great incentives for exporters to sue. Third, interested parties may accept Commission decisions for fear of retribution by the Commission in future investigations.

In short, even though great trade liberalisation and improvement in general public governance have been achieved since the end of the apartheid era in South Africa, it appears that more efforts still need to be made to ensure and promote transparency, stakeholders participation and the compliance with laws by authorities in the AD investigation and final decision-making process.

In summary, both emerging economies and industrial countries are subject to the *WTO AD Agreement* and suffer basically equally as a result of the substantive defects in the AD instrument. However, as shown by China's and South Africa's experience, poor governance in emerging economies' AD decision making, i.e., the low procedural requirements for their AD institutions, allows domestic producers to readily exploit these substantive defects to the largest extent possible. This in turn leads to the arbitrary and prolific use of AD on a scale disproportionate to such economies' share of total imports in the world.

1. For example, the AD *Regulations* provide that parties must be informed six months prior to the lapse of AD duties and that parties then have 30 days to request a review, with additional time to complete the sunset review questionnaire. However, in practice the Commission simply publishes a single list of lapsing duties in May the preceding year (Brink 2005:150–1).
2. Sections 46 and 47 of the *ITA Act* and Section 64 of the *AD Regulations*.
3. *Chairman of the Board v. Brenco* 2001 (4) AS 511 (SCA).

4. Conclusions

In the first section, this paper reveals that the AD instrument, while ostensibly aiming at offsetting unfair and anti-competitive trade practices, is actually deliberately designed to protect inefficient domestic producers from foreign competition, irrespective of the huge cost of such protection to the economy as a whole. AD has little in common with competition laws and can by no means be incorporated into the latter. AD enjoys broad political support in practice, due merely to the significant information-, incentive- and political influence-asymmetries between the lay public and well-organised producers in trade policy campaigns. It will be in the interests of all WTO members for the AD instrument to be completely removed. However, this best option has been ruled out in the WTO Doha Ministerial Declaration, which precludes any material reform of the *AD Agreement*. Therefore, procedural improvements in the formulation of national authorities' AD decisions are proposed in section 3 as the second best option. This section notes that both emerging economies and industrial countries are subject to the *WTO AD Agreement* and basically suffer equally under its substantive defects, but that it is the former that now account for a disproportionately large share of AD activity relative to their small imports. The paper then goes on to examine the AD institutions in China and South Africa, two major targets of AD and prolific new AD users. Three criteria of good governance are used in this analysis, namely transparency, stakeholder participation and the rule of law. It is argued, based on China's and South Africa's experience, that poor governance in emerging economies' AD decision-making allows domestic producers to easily use the substantive defects in the AD instrument to the greatest extent possible and thereby encourage the arbitrary and prolific use of AD by these relatively small importers. Emerging economies already maintain higher tariff barriers than industrial countries. Without effective steps to ensure better governance to restrain the arbitrary and proliferating use of AD, the benefits of the trade liberalisation for which they have been striving for decades may be largely squandered.

References

Bagwell, K. and R.W. Staiger (1999) 'An Economic Theory of GATT', *American Economic Review*, Vol. 89, pp. 215–48.

____ (2002) 'Economic Theory and the Interpretation of GATT/WTO', *American Economist*, Vol. 46, Iss. 2, pp. 3–20.

Bhagwati, J. (1989) *Protectionism.* Cambridge MA and London: MIT Press.

Baldwin, R.E. (1984) 'Rent-seeking and Trade Policy: An Industrial Approach', *Weltwirtschaftliches Archiv*, Vol. 120, pp. 662–77.

Baldwin, R.E. and M.O. Moore (1991) 'Political Aspects of the Administration of Trade Remedy Laws', in R. Boltuck and R. E. Litan (eds), *Down in the Dumps: Administration of the Unfair Trade Laws.* Washington, DC: Brookings Institute.

Bastiat, F. [1848] (1995) *Selected Essays on Political Economy.* New York: Foundation for Economic Education.

Belli, P., F. Michael and A. Ballivan (1993) 'South Africa: a Review of Trade Policies', *Informal Discussion Paper on Aspects of the Economy of South Africa* No. 4. Washington, DC: World Bank.

Blonigen, B. and C. Bown (2003) 'Antidumping and Retaliation Threats', *Journal of International Economics,* Vol. 60, pp. 249–73.

Blonigen, B. and T. Prusa (2004) 'Antidumping', in *Handbook of International Economics.* Oxford: Blackwell.

Brink, G. (2006) 'Proposed Amendments to the Anti-Dumping Regulations: Are the Amendments in Order?', *Tralac Working Paper* No. 21. Stellenbosch: US Printers.

Brink, G. (2005) 'The 10 Major Problems with the Anti-Dumping Instrument in South Africa', *Journal of World Trade*, Vol. 39, No. 1, pp. 147–57.

Buchanan, J. (1980) 'Rent Seeking and Profit Seeking', in J. Buchanan, R. Tollison, and G. Tullock (eds), *Toward a Theory of the Rent-seeking Society*, pp. 3–15. College Station: Texas A&M Press.

Business Monitor International (2008a) *The China Chemicals Report.* London: Business Monitor International.

_____ (2008a) *The South Africa Chemicals Report.* London: Business Monitor International.

Casson, A.C. and N.J. Reynolds (2006) 'Judicial Review of the International Trade Commission's Injury Determinations in Antidumping and Countervailing Duty Proceedings: An Overview and Analysis of Federal Court Decisions in 2005', *Georgetown Journal of International Law*, Vol. 38, No. 1, pp. 89–122.

Clark, D.S. (1995) 'The Robinson-Patman Act: General Principles, Commission Proceedings, and Selected Issues', Speech of the Secretary of Federal Trade Commission, available at http://www.ftc.gov/speeches/other/patman.shtm, last visited on 1 Jan 2008.

Corder, H. (2004) 'Judicial Authority in a Changing South Africa', *Legal Studies*, Vol. 24, Iss. 1–2, pp. 253–74.

Corr, C.F. (1997) 'Trade Protection in the New Millennium: The Ascendancy of Antidumping Measures', *Northwestern Journal of International Law and Business,* 18(1):49–110.

De Lange, R. (2003) *Business Guide to Trade Remedies in South Africa and the Southern African Customs Union: Anti-Dumping, Countervailing and Safeguards Legislation, Practices and Procedures.* Geneva: International Trade Centre.

Destler, I.M. (2005) *American Trade Politics*. 4th ed., Washington, DC: Institute for International Economics.
DeVault, J. (1990) 'The Administration of US Antidumping Duties: Some Empirical Observations', *World Economy*, Vol. 13, pp. 75–88.
Dornbusch, R., S. Fischer and P.A. Samuelson (1977) 'Comparative Advantage, Trade, and Payments in a Ricardian Model with a Continuum of Goods', *American Economic Review*, Vol. 67, pp. 823–39.
Downs, A. (1957) *An Economic Theory of Democracy*. New York: Harper and Row.
Edwards, L. and R. Lawrence (2008) 'SACU Tariff Policies: Where Should They Go From Here?', *Harvard CID Working Paper* No. 169, available at http://www.cid.harvard.edu/cidwp/, last visited on 16 Jun 2008.
European Commission (2006a) *Green Paper: European Transparency Initiative*, COM (2006) 194 final.
European Commission (2006b) *Green Paper on Trade Defence Instruments*, COM (2006) 763 final.
Eymann, A. and L. Schuknecht (1996) 'Antidumping Policy in the European Community: Political Discretion or Technical Determination?' *Economics and Politics*, 8, 111–31.
Feaver, D. (1997) 'A Regulatory Analysis of Australia's Antidumping Law and Policy: Statutory Failure or Regulatory Capture?', *Australian Journal of Public Administration*, 56, 67–77.
Feinberg, R. and K. Reynolds (2006) 'The Spread of Antidumping Regimes and the Role of Retaliation in Filings', *Southern Economic Journal*, Vol. 72, pp. 877–90.
Finger, J.M. and K.C. Fung (1994) 'Will GATT Enforcement Control Antidumping?', *Journal of Economic Integration*, 9, 198–213.
Finger, J.M., H.K. Hall and D.R. Nelson (1982) 'The Political Economy of Administered Protection', *American Economic Review*, Vol. 72, pp. 452–66.
Finger, J.M. and A. Zlate (2005) 'Antidumping: Prospects for Discipline from the Doha Negotiations', *Boston College Working Papers in Economics* No. 632, Boston College Department of Economics.
Freedom House (2007) Freedom in the World 2007. Washington, DC: Freedom House.
Friedman, M. (1962) *Capitalism and Freedom*. Chicago and London: University of Chicago Press.
Gilpin, R. (2000) *The Challenge of Global Capitalism*. Princeton: Princeton University Press.
Griswold, D. (2005) 'Four Decades of Failure: The US Embargo against Cuba', available at http://www.freetrade.org/node/433, last visited on 1 Jan 2008.
— (2004) 'Trading Tyranny for Freedom: How Open Markets Till the Soil for Democracy', *CATO Institute Trade Policy Analysis Paper* No. 26, available at http://www.freetrade.org/node/37, last visited on 1 Jan 2008.
Groombridge, M.A. (2000) 'China's Long March to a Market Economy: The Case for Permanent Normal Trade Relations with the People's Republic of China', *CATO Institute Trade Policy Analysis Paper* No. 10.
Hadar, L.T. (1998) 'US Sanctions Against Burma: A Failure on All Fronts', *CATO Institute Trade Policy Analysis Paper* No. 1, available at http://www.freetrade.org/node/62, last visited on 1 Jan 2008.
Harding, T. and J. Rattso (2005) 'The Barrier Model of Productivity Growth: South Africa', *Trade and Industry Policy Strategies Working Paper* No. 5.
Hayek, F.A. [1968] (1978) *New Studies in Philosophy, Politics, Economics and the History of Ideas*. Chicago: University of Chicago Press.

Hoekman, B. and P.C. Mavroidis (1996) 'Dumping, Antidumping and Antitrust', *Journal of World Trade*, Vol. 30, pp. 27–52.
Holden, M. (2002) 'Antidumping: A Reaction to Trade Liberalisation or Anti-Competitive?', *South African Journal of Economics*, Vol. 70, No. 5, pp. 912–31.
Horlick, G.N. (2005) 'The 10 Major Problems with the Anti-Dumping Instrument in the United States', *Journal of World Trade*, Vol. 39, No. 1, pp. 169–79.
Horlick, G.N. and Shea E.C. (1995) 'The World Trade Organization antidumping agreement', *Journal of World Trade*, Vol. 29, No. 1, pp. 5–31.
Hufbauer, G. and K. Elliott (1994) *Measuring the Costs of Protection in the United States.* Washington, DC: Institute for International Economics.
International Trade Administration Commission of South Africa (2005) Annual Report 2004/05, available online at http://www.itac.org.za/search.asp?search=annual+report, last visited on 1 Jul 2008.
International Trade Administration Commission of South Africa (2007) Annual Report 2006/07, available online at http://www.itac.org.za/search.asp?search=annual+report, last visited on 1 Jul 2008.
Jones, J.M. Jr. (1934) Tariff Retaliation: Repercussions of the Hawley-Smoot Bill. Philadelphia: University of Pennsylvania Press.
Jonsson, G. and A. Subramanian (2001) 'Dynamic Gains from Trade: Evidence from SA', *IMF Staff Paper* No. 48, 1, pp. 197–224.
Kaufmann, D, A. Kraay and M. Mastruzzi (2008) 'Governance Matters VII: Aggregate and Individual Governance Indicators, 1996–2007', *World Bank Policy Research Working Paper* No. 4654.
Keynes, J.M. ([1936] 2007) *The General Theory of Employment, Interest and Money.* London: Macmillan.
Knoll, M.S. (1991) 'Dump Our Anti-Dumping Law', *CATO Institute* Foreign Policy Briefing No. 11, available at http://www.cato.org/pub_display.php?pub_id=1536&full=1, last visited on 1 Jan 2008.
Krueger, A. (1974) 'The Political Economy of the Rent-Seeking Society', *American Economic Review*, Vol. 64, No. 2, pp. 291–303.
Kufuor, K.O. (1998) 'The Developing Countries and the Shaping of GATT/WTO Antidumping Law', *Journal of World Trade*, Vol. 32, No. 6, pp. 167–96.
Lamb, R.L. (2006) 'Rent Seeking in US Mexican Avocado Trade', *CATO Journal*, Vol. 26, No. 1, pp. 159–77.
Lindsey, L. and D.J. Ikenson (2003) *Antidumping Exposed: The Devilish Details of Unfair Trade Law.* Washington, DC: CATO Institute.
Lloyd, R., J. Oatham and M. Hammer (2007) 2007 Global Accountability Report. London: One World Trust.
Martins, S. (1999) 'Trade and Competition: An Industrial Economist's Perspective', *The World Economy*, Vol. 22, No. 6, pp. 895–907.
Mastel, G. (1998) *Antidumping Laws and the US Economy*, New York and London: Economic Strategy Institute.
McCarthy, C. (2005) 'Antidumping in South Africa', in National Board of Trade, Sweden: Report: *The Use of Antidumping in Brazil, China, India and South Africa.*
McCarthy, C. (1988) 'Structural Development of South African Manufacturing Industry – A Policy Perspective', *South African Journal of Economics*, Vol. 56, pp. 1–23.
Messerlin, P. (2004) 'China in the World Trade Organization: Antidumping and Safeguards', *World Bank Economic Review*, Vol. 18, No.1, pp. 105–30.

Messerlin, P. (1994) 'Should Antidumping Rules be Replaced by National or International Competition Rules?', *Aussenwirtschaft*, Vol. 49, pp. 351–74.

Mill, J.S. [1848] (1965) *Principles of Political Economy with Some of Their Applications to Social Philosophy*, Book III. Toronto: University of Toronto Press.

Mises, L.V. [1949] (1998) *Human Action*, 4th ed. Irvington: Foundation for Economic Education.

Mises, L.V. (1944) *Omnipotent Government*. New Haven: Yale University Press.

Moore, M. and M. Zanardi (2006) 'Does Antidumping Use Contribute to Trade Liberalization? An Empirical Analysis', *CentER working paper* No. 61.

Mueller, D.C. (1991) 'Choosing a Constitution in East Europe: Lessons from Public Choice', *Journal of Comparative Economics*, Vol. 15, pp. 325–48.

Nelson, D.R. (2006) 'Proliferation of Contingent Protection among Developing Countries: Causes and Consequences', available at http://www.tulane.edu/~dnelson/PAPERS/ADinLDCsFinal.pdf, lasted visited on 3 Dec. 2007.

Niels, Gunnar and A. ten Kate (2006) 'Antidumping Policy in Developing Countries: Safety Valve or Obstacle to Free Trade?', *European Journal of Political Economy*, Vol. 22, No. 3, pp. 618–38.

ODI (2006), "Governance, Development and Aid Effectiveness: A Quick Guide to Complex Relationships". Available online at http://www.odi.org.uk/publications/briefing/bp_mar06_governance.pdf, last visited: 3 May 2007.

OECD (2005) *Governance in China*, Paris: OECD.

OECD (2002) *Governance for Sustainable Development: Five OECD Case Studies*. Paris: OECD.

OECD (1997), 'Final Report of the Ad Hoc Working Group on Participatory Development and Good Governance', *Development Cooperation Guidelines Series*. Available online at http://www.oecd.org/dataoecd/44/12/1894642.pdf, last visited: 3 Jul 2007.

Olson, M. (1965) *The Logic of Collective Action*. Cambridge MA: Harvard University Press.

Palmeter, D. (1995) 'United States Implementation of the Uruguay Round Antidumping Code', *Journal of World Trade*, 29(3): 39–82.

Prusa, T. (1992) 'Why are So Many Antidumping Petitions Withdrawn?', *Journal of International Economics*, Vol. 33, pp. 1–20.

Prusa, T.J. and S. Skeath (2002) 'The Economic and Strategic Motives for Antidumping Filings', *Weltwirtschaftliches Archiv*, Vol. 138, pp. 389–413.

Ricardo, D. (1821) *On the Principles of Political Economy and Taxation*, 3rd ed. London: John Murray, available online at http://www.econlib.org/library/Ricardo/ricP.html, last visited: 4 Apr 2008.

Rosen, S.M. and G. Husisian (2006) 'Judicial Review by the US Court of International Trade and the US Court of Appeals for the Federal Circuit under 19 USC. §1581(c) of Antidumping and Countervailing Duty Determinations Issued by the Department of Commerce', *Georgetown Journal of International Law*, Vol. 38, No. 1, pp. 39–88.

Rothbard, M. [1962] (2004) *Man, Economy, and State*, 2nd ed. Auburn: Ludwig von Mises Institute.

Rowley, C.K., W. Thorbecke and R.E. Wagner (1995) *Trade Protection in the United States*. Aldershot (UK) and Brookfield (US): Edward Elgar.

Samuelson, P. and W. Nordhaus (1998) *Economics*, 16th ed. New York: McGraw Hill.

Schattschneider, E.E. (1935) *Politics, Pressures and the Tariff.* New York: Prentice Hall.

Schumpeter, J. (1943) *Capitalism, Socialism and Democracy*. London: George Allen and Unwin.

Sen, A. (1981) *Poverty and Famines: An Essay on Entitlement and Deprivation*. Oxford: Clarendon Press.

Smith, A. [1776] (1947) *An Inquiry into the Nature and Causes of the Wealth of Nations*, London: Dent.

Stegemann, K. (1990) 'EC Anti-dumping Policy: Are Price Undertakings a Legal Substitute for Illegal Price Fixing?', *Weltwirtschaftliches Archiv*, Vol. 126, pp. 268–97.

Stigler, G. (1976) 'Do Economists Matter?', *Southern Economic Journal*, Vol. 42, No. 3, pp. 347–54.

Stigler, G. (1975) *The Citizen and the State: Essays on Regulation*. Chicago: University of Chicago Press.

Stigler, G. (1971) 'The Theory of Economic Regulation', *Bell Journal of Economics*, Vol. 2, pp. 3–21.

Stiglitz, J. (2006), *Making Globalization Work*, London: Penguin.

Stiglitz, J. (1996) 'Some Lessons from the East Asian Miracle', *World Bank Research Observer*, Vol. 11, No. 2, pp. 151–77.

Stokes, B. and P. Choate. (2001) Democratizing US Trade Policy. New York: Council on Foreign Relations.

Tobin, J. (1995) 'Democratic Values and Capitalist Efficiency: The Liberal Reconciliation', in W.L. Taitte (ed.) *Moral Values in Liberalism and Conservatism*. Austin: University of Texas Press.

Tobin, J. (1981) 'Nobel Lecture: Money and Finance in the Macroeconomic Process', *Journal of Money, Credit and Banking*, Vol. 14, No. 2, pp. 171–204.

Trebilock, M. and R. Howse (1999) *The Regulation of International Trade*. London: Routledge.

Tullock, G. (1996) 'Corruption Theory and Practice', *Contemporary Economic Policy*, Vol. 14, No. 3, pp. 6–13.

Tullock, G. (1974) 'More on the Welfare Cost of Transfers', *Kyklos Fasc*, Vol. 2, pp. 378–81.

Turgot, A. [1774] *Reflections on the Production and Distribution of Wealth*, in P.D. Groenewegen (1977) *The Economics of A.R.J. Turgot*. The Hague: Martinus Nijhoff.

UNDP (2007), *Governance Indicators: A User's Guide* (2nd *ed.*). Available online at http://www.undp.org/oslocentre/docs07/undp_users_guide_online_version.pdf, last visited: 8 Jun 2007.

UNDP (1999), *Governance for Sustainable Human Development – A UNDP Policy Document*, New York. Available online at http://mirror.undp.org/magnet/policy/default.htm, last visited 7 Jun 2007.

UNESCAP (2007), *What is Good Governance?*. Available online at http://www.unescap.org/pdd/prs/ProjectActivities/Ongoing/gg/governance.asp, last visited: 7 Jan 2007.

USTR (2008) National Trade Estimate Report on Foreign Trade Barriers 2008. Washington DC: USTR.

Vandenbussche, H. and M. Zanardi (2008) 'What Explains the Proliferation of Antidumping laws?', *Economic Policy*, Vol. 23, Iss. 53, pp. 93–138.

Vandenbussche, H. and M. Zanardi (2007) 'The Global Chilling Effects of Antidumping Proliferation', *CEPR Discussion Paper* 5597, revised and resubmitted to *Journal of International Economics*.

Vermulst, E. and B. Driessen (1997) 'New Battle Lines in the Anti-Dumping War'. *Journal of World Trade. June*, 31(3) pp. 135–59.

Waer, P. (1993) 'Constructed Normal Values in EC Dumping Margin Calculations. Fiction, or a Realistic Approach?', *Journal of World Trade*, 27(4):47–80.

White, J. J. (1997) 'A Test of Consistency in the Administration of US Antidumping Law', *Journal of World Trade*, 31(4):117–28.

Wooton, I. and M. Zanardi (2002) '*Trade and Competition Policy: Anti-Dumping versus Anti-Trust*', available at: http://homepages.srath.ac.uk/~hbs03116/Research/Trade%20and%20Competition%20Policy%20Final.pdf, last visited on 1Jul 2008.

World Bank (2000) *Reforming Public Institutions and Strengthening Governance*, World Bank Strategy Paper, Washington DC: World Bank.

World Bank (1998) *Assessing Aid: What Works, What Doesn't and Why?* Washington DC: World Bank.

World Bank (1992), *Governance and Development*, Washington DC: World Bank.

WTO (2008) *Trade Policy Review Report (China 2008)*, by the WTO General Secretariat, WT/TPR/S/199.

WTO (2007) *Draft Consolidated Chair Texts of the AD and SCM Agreements*, TN/RL/W/213.

WTO (2006) *Trade Policy Review Report (China 2006)*, by the WTO General Secretariat, WT/TPR/S/161.

WTO (2003) *Committee on Anti-Dumping Practices – Committee on Subsidies and Countervailing Measures – Notifications of Laws and Regulations under Article 18.5 and Article 32.6 of the Agreements: Replies to Questions posed by the United States 1 and Regarding the Notification of China 2*, G/ADP/Q1/CHN/33; G/SCM/Q1/CHN/33.

WTO (2002a) *Negotiating Group on Rules – Communication from the United States – Basic Concepts and Principles of the Trade Remedy Rules*, TN/RL/W/27.

WTO (2002b) *Negotiating Group on Rules – Investigatory Procedures under the Anti-Dumping and Subsidies Agreements – Submission by the United States* TN/RL/W/35.

WTO (2001) *Doha Ministerial Declaration*, WT/MIN(01)/DEC/1.

WTO (1998) *Working Group on the Interaction between Trade and Competition Policy – Communication from the United States*, WT/WGTCP/W/88.

Yu, T. (2005) 'The 10 Major Problems with the Anti-Dumping Instrument in the People's Republic of China', *Journal of World Trade*, Vol. 39, No. 1, pp. 97–103.

DISCUSSION PAPERS PUBLISHED BY THE INSTITUTE

Recent issues in the series are available electronically for downloading free of charge

www.nai.uu.se

1. Kenneth Hermele and Bertil Odén, *Sanctions and Dilemmas. Some Implications of Economic Sanctions against South Africa.* 1988. 43 pp. ISBN 91-7106-286-6
2. Elling Njål Tjönneland, *Pax Pretoriana. The Fall of Apartheid and the Politics of Regional Destabilisation.* 1989. 31 pp. ISBN 91-7106-292-0
3. Hans Gustafsson, Bertil Odén and Andreas Tegen, *South African Minerals. An Analysis of Western Dependence.* 1990. 47 pp. ISBN 91-7106-307-2
4. Bertil Egerö, *South African Bantustans. From Dumping Grounds to Battlefronts.* 1991. 46 pp. ISBN 91-7106-315-3
5. Carlos Lopes, *Enough is Enough! For an Alternative Diagnosis of the African Crisis.* 1994. 38 pp. ISBN 91-7106-347-1
6. Annika Dahlberg, *Contesting Views and Changing Paradigms.* 1994. 59 pp. ISBN 91-7106-357-9,
7. Bertil Odén, *Southern African Futures. Critical Factors for Regional Development in Southern Africa.* 1996. 35 pp. ISBN 91-7106-392-7
8. Colin Leys and Mahmood Mamdani, *Crisis and Reconstruction – African Perspectives.* 1997. 26 pp. ISBN 91-7106-417-6
9. Gudrun Dahl, *Responsibility and Partnership in Swedish Aid Discourse.* 2001. 30 pp. ISBN 91-7106-473-7
10. Henning Melber and Christopher Saunders, *Transition in Southern Africa – Comparative Aspects.* 2001. 28 pp. ISBN 91-7106-480-X
11. *Regionalism and Regional Integration in Africa.*2001. 74 pp. ISBN 91-7106-484-2
12. Souleymane Bachir Diagne, et al., *Identity and Beyond: Rethinking Africanity.* 2001. 33 pp. ISBN 91-7106-487-7
13. Georges Nzongola-Ntalaja, et al., *Africa in the New Millennium.* Edited by Raymond Suttner. 2001. 53 pp. ISBN 91-7106-488-5
14. *Zimbabwe's Presidential Elections 2002.* Edited by Henning Melber. 2002. 88 pp. ISBN 91-7106-490-7
15. Birgit Brock-Utne, *Language, Education and Democracy in Africa.* 2002. 47 pp. ISBN 91-7106-491-5
16. Henning Melber et al., *The New Partnership for Africa's development (NEPAD).* 2002. 36 pp. ISBN 91-7106-492-3
17. Juma Okuku, *Ethnicity, State Power and the Democratisation Process in Uganda.* 2002. 42 pp. ISBN 91-7106-493-1
18. Yul Derek Davids, et al., *Measuring Democracy and Human Rights in Southern Africa.* Compiled by Henning Melber. 2002. 50 pp. ISBN 91-7106-497-4
19. Michael Neocosmos, Raymond Suttner and Ian Taylor, *Political Cultures in Democratic South Africa.* Compiled by Henning Melber. 2002. 52 pp. ISBN 91-7106-498-2
20. Martin Legassick, *Armed Struggle and Democracy. The Case of South Africa.* 2002. 53 pp. ISBN 91-7106-504-0
21. Reinhart Kössler, Henning Melber and Per Strand, *Development from Below. A Namibian Case Study.* 2003. 32 pp. ISBN 91-7106-507-5
22. Fred Hendricks, *Fault-Lines in South African Democracy. Continuing Crises of Inequality and Injustice.* 2003. 32 pp. ISBN 91-7106-508-3
23. Kenneth Good, *Bushmen and Diamonds. (Un)Civil Society in Botswana.* 2003. 39 pp. ISBN 91-7106-520-2
24. Robert Kappel, Andreas Mehler, Henning Melber and Anders Danielson, *Structural Stability in an African Context.* 2003. 55 pp. ISBN 91-7106-521-0
25. Patrick Bond, *South Africa and Global Apartheid. Continental and International Policies and Politics.* 2004. 45 pp. ISBN 91-7106-523-7

26. Bonnie Campbell (ed.), *Regulating Mining in Africa. For whose benefit?* 2004. 89 pp. ISBN 91-7106-527-X
27. Suzanne Dansereau and Mario Zamponi, *Zimbabwe – The Political Economy of Decline.* Compiled by Henning Melber. 2005. 43 pp. ISBN 91-7106-541-5
28. Lars Buur and Helene Maria Kyed, *State Recognition of Traditional Authority in Mozambique. The nexus of Community Representation and State Assistance.* 2005. 30 pp. ISBN 91-7106-547-4
29. Hans Eriksson and Björn Hagströmer, *Chad – Towards Democratisation or Petro-Dictatorship?* 2005. 82 pp. ISBN 91-7106-549-0
30. Mai Palmberg and Ranka Primorac (eds), *Skinning the Skunk – Facing Zimbabwean Futures.* 2005. 40 pp. ISBN 91-7106-552-0
31. Michael Brüntrup, Henning Melber and Ian Taylor, *Africa, Regional Cooperation and the World Market – Socio-Economic Strategies in Times of Global Trade Regimes.* Compiled by Henning Melber. 2006. 70 pp. ISBN 91-7106-559-8
32. Fibian Kavulani Lukalo, *Extended Handshake or Wrestling Match? – Youth and Urban Culture Celebrating Politics in Kenya.* 2006. 58 pp. ISBN 91-7106-567-9
33. Tekeste Negash, *Education in Ethiopia: From Crisis to the Brink of Collapse.* 2006. 55 pp. ISBN 91-7106-576-8
34. Fredrik Söderbaum and Ian Taylor (eds) *Micro-Regionalism in West Africa. Evidence from Two Case Studies.* 2006. 32 pp. ISBN 91-7106-584-9
35. Henning Melber (ed.), *On Africa – Scholars and African Studies.* 2006. 68 pp. ISBN 978-91-7106-585-8
36. Amadu Sesay, *Does One Size Fit All? The Sierra Leone Truth and Reconciliation Commission Revisited.* 2007. 56 pp. ISBN 978-91-7106-586-5
37. Karolina Hulterström, Amin Y. Kamete and Henning Melber, *Political Opposition in African Countries – The Case of Kenya, Namibia, Zambia and Zimbabwe.* 2007. 86 pp. ISBN 978-7106-587-2
38. Henning Melber (ed.), *Governance and State Delivery in Southern Africa. Examples from Botswana, Namibia and Zimbabwe.* 2007. 65 pp. ISBN 978-91-7106-587-2
39. Cyril Obi (ed.), *Perspectives on Côte d'Ivoire: Between Political Breakdown and Post-Conflict Peace.* 2007. 66 pp. ISBN 978-91-7106-606-6
40. Anna Chitando, *Imagining a Peaceful Society. A Vision of Children's Literature in a Post-Conflict Zimbabwe.* 2008. 26 pp. ISBN 978-91-7106-623-7
41. Olawale Ismail, *The Dynamics of Post-Conflict Reconstruction and Peace Building in West Africa. Between Change and Stability.* 2009. 52 pp. ISBN 978-91-7106-637-4
42. Ron Sandrey and Hannah Edinger, *Examining the South Africa–China Agricultural Relationship.* 2009. 58 pp. ISBN 978-91-7106-643-5
43. Xuan Gao, *The Proliferation of Anti-Dumping and Poor Governance in Emerging Economies.* 2009. 41 pp. ISBN 978-91-644-2

www.ingramcontent.com/pod-product-compliance
Ingram Content Group UK Ltd.
Pitfield, Milton Keynes, MK11 3LW, UK
UKHW061657190726
13853UKWH00008B/2259

9 789171 066442